THE WASTE LAND

BY

T. S. ELIOT

"NAM Sibyllam quidem Cumis ego ipse oculis meis
vidi in ampulla pendere, et cum illi pueri dicerent:
Σίβυλλα τί θέλεις; respondebat illa: ἀποθανεῖν θέλω."

Martino Publishing
Mansfield Centre, CT
2013

Martino Publishing
P.O. Box 373,
Mansfield Centre, CT 06250 USA

ISBN 978-1-61427-431-5

© *2013 Martino Publishing*

Cover design by T. Matarazzo

Printed in the United States of America On 100% Acid-Free Paper

THE WASTE LAND

BY

T. S. ELIOT

"NAM Sibyllam quidem Cumis ego ipse oculis meis
vidi in ampulla pendere, et cum illi pueri dicerent:
Σίβυλλα τί θέλεις; respondebat illa: ἀποθανεῖν θέλω."

NEW YORK
BONI AND LIVERIGHT

THE WASTE LAND

I. THE BURIAL OF THE DEAD

APRIL is the cruellest month, breeding
Lilacs out of the dead land, mixing
Memory and desire, stirring
Dull roots with spring rain.
Winter kept us warm, covering
Earth in forgetful snow, feeding
A little life with dried tubers.
Summer surprised us, coming over the
    Starnbergersee
With a shower of rain; we stopped in the
    colonnade,
And went on in sunlight, into the Hof-
    garten,   10

And drank coffee, and talked for an hour.

Bin gar keine Russin, stamm' aus Litauen,

    echt deutsch.

And when we were children, staying at the

    archduke's,

My cousin's, he took me out on a sled,

And I was frightened. He said, Marie,

Marie, hold on tight. And down we went.

In the mountains, there you feel free.

I read, much of the night, and go south

    in the winter.

What are the roots that clutch, what

    branches grow

Out of this stony rubbish? Son of

    man,   20

You cannot say, or guess, for you know
    only
A heap of broken images, where the sun
    beats,
And the dead tree gives no shelter, the
    cricket no relief,
And the dry stone no sound of water.   Only
There is shadow under this red rock,
(Come in under the shadow of this red
    rock),
And I will show you something different
    from either
Your shadow at morning striding behind
    you
Or your shadow at evening rising to meet
    you;

I will show you fear in a handful of

dust.   30

> *Frisch weht der Wind*
> *Der Heimat zu,*
> *Mein Irisch Kind,*
> *Wo weilest du?*

"You gave me hyacinths first a year ago;

"They called me the hyacinth girl."

— Yet when we came back, late, from the

    Hyacinth garden,

Your arms full, and your hair wet, I

    could not

Speak, and my eyes failed, I was neither

Living nor dead, and I knew nothing,   40

Looking into the heart of light, the

    silence.

Od' und leer das Meer.

Madame Sosostris, famous clairvoyante,

Had a bad cold, nevertheless

Is known to be the wisest woman in

   Europe,

With a wicked pack of cards. Here, said

   she,

Is your card, the drowned Phoenician

   Sailor,

(Those are pearls that were his eyes.

   Look !)

Here is Belladonna, the Lady of the Rocks,

The lady of situations.   50

Here is the man with three staves, and

   here the Wheel,

And here is the one-eyed merchant, and
   this card,
Which is blank, is something he carries on
   his back,
Which I am forbidden to see.   I do not
   find
The Hanged Man.   Fear death by water.
I see crowds of people, walking round in
   a ring.
Thank you.   If you see dear Mrs. Equi-
   tone,
Tell her I bring the horoscope myself:
One must be so careful these days.

Unreal City,   60
Under the brown fog of a winter dawn,

A crowd flowed over London Bridge, so
 many,
I had not thought death had undone so
 many.
Sighs, short and infrequent, were exhaled,
And each man fixed his eyes before his feet.
Flowed up the hill and down King William
 Street,
To where Saint Mary Woolnoth kept the
 hours
With a dead sound on the final stroke of
 nine.
There I saw one I knew, and stopped him,
 crying: "Stetson!
"You who were with me in the ships at
 Mylae!   70

"That corpse you planted last year in
    your garden,
"Has it begun to sprout? Will it bloom
    this year?
"Or has the sudden frost disturbed its
    bed?
"Oh keep the Dog far hence, that's friend
    to men,
"Or with his nails he'll dig it up again!
"You! hypocrite lecteur! — mon sem-
    blable, — mon frère!"

II. A GAME OF CHESS

THE Chair she sat in, like a bur-
    nished throne,
Glowed on the marble, where the glass
Held up by standards wrought with
    fruited vines
From which a golden Cupidon peeped
    out   80
(Another hid his eyes behind his wing)
Doubled the flames of sevenbranched
    candelabra
Reflecting light upon the table as
The glitter of her jewels rose to meet it,
From satin cases poured in rich profusion;

In vials of ivory and coloured glass
Unstoppered, lurked her strange synthetic
    perfumes,
Unguent, powdered, or liquid — troubled,
    confused
And drowned the sense in odours; stirred
    by the air
That freshened from the window, these
    ascended   90
In fattening the prolonged candle-flames,
Flung their smoke into the laquearia,
Stirring the pattern on the coffered ceiling.
Huge sea-wood fed with copper
Burned green and orange, framed by the
    coloured stone,
In which sad light a carved dolphin swam.

A GAME OF CHESS

Above the antique mantel was displayed

As though a window gave upon the sylvan
  scene

The change of Philomel, by the barbarous
  king

So rudely forced; yet there the nightin-
  gale   100

Filled all the desert with inviolable voice

And still she cried, and still the world
  pursues,

"Jug Jug" to dirty ears.

And other withered stumps of time

Were told upon the walls; staring forms

Leaned out, leaning, hushing the room
  enclosed.

Footsteps shuffled on the stair.

Under the firelight, under the brush, her
hair
Spread out in fiery points
Glowed into words, then would be sav-
agely still.   110

"My nerves are bad tonight. Yes, bad.
Stay with me.
"Speak to me. Why do you never speak.
Speak.
"What are you thinking of? What think-
ing? What?
"I never know what you are thinking.
Think."

I think we are in rats' alley
Where the dead men lost their bones.

"What is that noise?"

              The wind under the door.

"What is that noise now? What is the
   wind doing?"

           Nothing again nothing.   120

                  "Do

"You know nothing? Do you see nothing?
   Do you remember

"Nothing?"

        I remember

Those are pearls that were his eyes.

"Are you alive, or not? Is there nothing
   in your head?"

                  But

O O O O that Shakespeherian Rag —
It's so elegant
So intelligent   130

"What shall I do now? What shall
I do?"
"I shall rush out as I am, and walk the
street
"With my hair down, so. What shall we
do tomorrow?
"What shall we ever do?"
                    The hot water at ten.
And if it rains, a closed car at four.
And we shall play a game of chess,
Pressing lidless eyes and waiting for a
knock upon the door.

When Lil's husband got demobbed, I
said —

I didn't mince my words, I said to her
    myself,   140
HURRY UP PLEASE ITS TIME
Now Albert's coming back, make your-
    self a bit smart.
He'll want to know what you done with
    that money he gave you
To get yourself some teeth. He did, I was
    there.
You have them all out, Lil, and get a
    nice set,
He said, I swear, I can't bear to look at you.
And no more can't I, I said, and think of
    poor Albert,
He's been in the army four years, he
    wants a good time,

[23]

And if you dont give it him, there's
   others will, I said.
Oh is there, she said. Something o' that,
   I said.   150
Then I'll know who to thank, she said,
   and give me a straight look.
HURRY UP PLEASE ITS TIME
If you dont like it you can get on with it,
   I said,
Others can pick and choose if you can't.
But if Albert makes off, it wont be for
   lack of telling.
You ought to be ashamed, I said, to look
   so antique.
(And her only thirty-one.)
I can't help it, she said, pulling a long face,

It's them pills I took, to bring it off, she
    said.
(She's had five already, and nearly died
    of young George.)   160
The chemist said it would be alright, but
    I've never been the same.
You *are* a proper fool, I said.
Well, if Albert wont leave you alone, there
    it is, I said,
What you get married for if you dont
    want children?
HURRY UP PLEASE ITS TIME
Well, that Sunday Albert was home, they
    had a hot gammon,
And they asked me in to dinner, to get
    the beauty of it hot —

HURRY UP PLEASE ITS TIME
HURRY UP PLEASE ITS TIME
Goonight Bill. Goonight Lou. Goonight
    May. Goonight.   170
Ta ta. Goonight. Goonight.
Good night, ladies, good night, sweet
    ladies, good night, good night.

III. THE FIRE SERMON

THE river's tent is broken: the last
fingers of leaf
Clutch and sink into the wet bank. The
wind
Crosses the brown land, unheard. The
nymphs are departed.
Sweet Thames, run softly, till I end my
song.
The river bears no empty bottles, sand-
wich papers,
Silk handkerchiefs, cardboard boxes, cigar-
ette ends
Or other testimony of summer nights.
The nymphs are departed.

And their friends, the loitering heirs of city

    directors;   180

Departed, have left no addresses.

By the waters of Leman I sat down and

    wept . . . .

Sweet Thames, run softly till I end my

    song,

Sweet Thames, run softly, for I speak not

    loud or long.

But at my back in a cold blast I hear

The rattle of the bones, and chuckle

    spread from ear to ear.

A rat crept softly through the vegetation

Dragging its slimy belly on the bank

While I was fishing in the dull canal

On a winter evening round behind the
  gashouse   190
Musing upon the king my brother's
  wreck
And on the king my father's death before
  him.
White bodies naked on the low damp
  ground
And bones cast in a little low dry garret,
Rattled by the rat's foot only, year to year.
But at my back from time to time I hear
The sound of horns and motors, which
  shall bring
Sweeney to Mrs. Porter in the spring.
O the moon shone bright on Mrs. Porter
And on her daughter   200

They wash their feet in soda water
Et O ces voix d'enfants, chantant dans la
  coupole!

Twit twit twit
Jug jug jug jug jug jug
So rudely forc'd.
Tereu

Unreal City
Under the brown fog of a winter noon
Mr. Eugenides, the Smyrna merchant
Unshaven, with a pocket full of currants 210
C.i.f. London: documents at sight,
Asked me in demotic French
To luncheon at the Cannon Street Hotel

Followed by a weekend at the Metropole.

At the violet hour, when the eyes and back
Turn upward from the desk, when the
     human engine waits
Like a taxi throbbing waiting,
I Tiresias, though blind, throbbing be-
     tween two lives,
Old man with wrinkled female breasts,
     can see
At the violet hour, the evening hour that
     strives   220
Homeward, and brings the sailor home
     from sea,
The typist home at teatime, clears her
     breakfast, lights

Her stove, and lays out food in tins.

Out of the window perilously spread

Her drying combinations touched by the
  sun's last rays,

On the divan are piled (at night her bed)

Stockings, slippers, camisoles, and stays.

I Tiresias, old man with wrinkled dugs

Perceived the scene, and foretold the rest —

I too awaited the expected guest.   230

He, the young man carbuncular, arrives,

A small house agent's clerk, with one bold
  stare,

One of the low on whom assurance sits

As a silk hat on a Bradford millionaire.

The time is now propitious, as he guesses,

The meal is ended, she is bored and tired,

Endeavours to engage her in caresses

Which still are unreproved, if undesired.

Flushed and decided, he assaults at once;

Exploring hands encounter no defence; 240

His vanity requires no response,

And makes a welcome of indifference.

(And I Tiresias have foresuffered all

Enacted on this same divan or bed;

I who have sat by Thebes below the wall

And walked among the lowest of the dead.)

Bestows one final patronising kiss,

And gropes his way, finding the stairs

    unlit . . .

She turns and looks a moment in the glass,

Hardly aware of her departed lover; 250

Her brain allows one half-formed thought
    to pass:
"Well now that's done: and I'm glad it's
    over."
When lovely woman stoops to folly and
Paces about her room again, alone,
She smoothes her hair with automatic hand,
And puts a record on the gramophone.

"This music crept by me upon the
    waters"
And along the Strand, up Queen Victoria
    Street.
O City city, I can sometimes hear
Beside a public bar in Lower Thames
    Street,   260

The pleasant whining of a mandoline

And a clatter and a chatter from within

Where fishmen lounge at noon: where the
walls

Of Magnus Martyr hold

Inexplicable splendour of Ionian white
and gold.

The river sweats

Oil and tar

The barges drift

With the turning tide

Red sails   270

Wide

To leeward, swing on the heavy spar.

The barges wash

Drifting logs

Down Greenwich reach

Past the Isle of Dogs.

      Weialala leia

      Wallala leialala

Elizabeth and Leicester

Beating oars   280

The stern was formed

A gilded shell

Red and gold

The brisk swell

Rippled both shores

Southwest wind

Carried down stream

The peal of bells

White towers

Weialala leia   290

Wallala leialala

"Trams and dusty trees.

Highbury bore me. Richmond and Kew

Undid me. By Richmond I raised my

knees

Supine on the floor of a narrow canoe."

"My feet are at Moorgate, and my heart

Under my feet. After the event

He wept. He promised 'a new start.'

I made no comment. What should I

resent?"

"On Margate Sands.   300

I can connect

Nothing with nothing.

[37]

The broken fingernails of dirty hands.
My people humble people who expect
Nothing."
                    la la

To Carthage then I came

Burning burning burning burning
O Lord Thou pluckest me out
O Lord Thou pluckest   310

burning

IV. DEATH BY WATER

PHLEBAS the Phoenician, a fortnight
    dead,
Forgot the cry of gulls, and the deep sea
    swell
And the profit and loss.
                A current under sea
Picked his bones in whispers. As he rose
    and fell
He passed the stages of his age and youth
Entering the whirlpool.
              Gentile or Jew
O you who turn the wheel and look to
    windward,   320
Consider Phlebas, who was once handsome
    and tall as you.

V. WHAT THE THUNDER SAID

AFTER the torchlight red on sweaty
faces

After the frosty silence in the gardens

After the agony in stony places

The shouting and the crying

Prison and palace and reverberation

Of thunder of spring over distant
mountains

He who was living is now dead

We who were living are now dying

With a little patience   30

Here is no water but only rock

Rock and no water and the sandy road

The road winding above among the
   mountains
Which are mountains of rock without
   water
If there were water we should stop and
   drink
Amongst the rock one cannot stop or
   think
Sweat is dry and feet are in the sand
If there were only water amongst the
   rock
Dead mount in mouth of carious teeth
   that cannot spit
Here one can neither stand nor lie nor sit 340
There is not even silence in the moun-
   tains

But dry sterile thunder without rain
There is not even solitude in the
mountains
But red sullen faces sneer and snarl
From doors of mudcracked houses

              If there were water

  And no rock

  If there were rock

  And also water

  And water

  A spring   350

  A pool among the rock

  If there were the sound of water only

  Not the cicada

  And dry grass singing

  But sound of water over a rock

WHAT THE THUNDER SAID

Where the hermit-thrush sings in the
  pine trees
Drip drop drip drop drop drop drop
But there is no water

Who is the third who walks always beside
  you?
When I count, there are only you and I
  together   360
But when I look ahead up the white road
There is always another one walking be-
  side you
Gliding wrapt in a brown mantle, hooded
I do not know whether a man or a woman
— But who is that on the other side of
  you?

What is that sound high in the air

Murmur of maternal lamentation

Who are those hooded hordes swarming

Over endless plains, stumbling in cracked
    earth

Ringed by the flat horizon only   370

What is the city over the mountains

Cracks and reforms and bursts in the violet
    air

Falling towers

Jerusalem Athens Alexandria

Vienna London

Unreal

A woman drew her long black hair out
    tight

And fiddled whisper music on those strings
And bats with baby faces in the violet light
Whistled, and beat their wings   380
And crawled head downward down a
    blackened wall
And upside down in air were towers
Tolling reminiscent bells, that kept the
    hours
And voices singing out of empty cisterns
    and exhausted wells.

In this decayed hole among the mountains
In the faint moonlight, the grass is singing
Over the tumbled graves, about the chapel
There is the empty chapel, only the wind's
    home.

It has no windows, and the door swings,

Dry bones can harm no one.   390

Only a cock stood on the rooftree

Co co rico co co rico

In a flash of lightning. Then a damp

　　gust

Bringing rain

Ganga was sunken, and the limp leaves

Waited for rain, while the black clouds

Gathered far distant, over Himavant.

The jungle crouched, humped in silence.

Then spoke the thunder

DA   400

Datta: what have we given?

My friend, blood shaking my heart

The awful daring of a moment's surrender

Which an age of prudence can never
    retract
By this, and this only, we have existed
Which is not to be found in our obituaries
Or in memories draped by the beneficent
    spider
Or under seals broken by the lean solicitor
In our empty rooms
Da   410
Dayadhvam: I have heard the key
Turn in the door once and turn once
    only
We think of the key, each in his prison
Thinking of the key, each confirms a
    prison
Only at nightfall, aetherial rumours

Revive for a moment a broken Coriolanus

DA

Damyata: The boat responded

Gaily, to the hand expert with sail and

    oar

The sea was calm, your heart would have

    responded   420

Gaily, when invited, beating obedient

To controlling hands

                I sat upon the shore

Fishing, with the arid plain behind me

Shall I at least set my lands in order?

London Bridge is falling down falling down

    falling down

WHAT THE THUNDER SAID

Poi s'ascose nel foco che gli affina

Quando fiam ceu chelidon — O swallow
   swallow

Le Prince d'Aquitaine à la tour abolie

These fragments I have shored against my
   ruins   430

Why then Ile fit you.   Hieronymo's mad
   againe.

Datta. Dayadhvam. Damyata.

   Shantih   shantih   shantih

NOTES

NOTES

NOTES

NOT only the title, but the plan and a good deal of the incidental symbolism of the poem were suggested by Miss Jessie L. Weston's book on the Grail legend: *From Ritual to Romance* (Macmillan). Indeed, so deeply am I indebted, Miss Weston's book will elucidate the difficulties of the poem much better than my notes can do; and I recommend it (apart from the great interest of the book itself) to any who think such elucidation of the poem worth the trouble. To another work of anthropology I am indebted in general, one which has influenced our generation profoundly; I mean *The Golden Bough;* I have used especially the two volumes *Atthis Adonis Osiris*. Anyone who is acquainted with these works will immediately recognise in the poem certain references to vegetation ceremonies.

I. THE BURIAL OF THE DEAD

Line 20. Cf. Ezekiel II, i.

23. Cf. Ecclesiastes XII, v.

31. V. Tristan und Isolde, I, verses 5–8.

42. Id. III, verse 24.

46. I am not familiar with the exact constitution of the Tarot pack of cards, from which I have obviously departed to suit my own convenience. The Hanged Man, a member of the traditional pack, fits my purpose in two ways: because he is associated in my mind with the Hanged God of Frazer, and because I associate him with the hooded figure in the passage of the disciples to Emmaus in Part V. The Phoenician Sailor and the Merchant appear later; also the "crowds of people," and Death by Water is executed in Part IV. The Man with Three Staves (an authentic member of the Tarot pack) I associate, quite arbitrarily, with the Fisher King himself.

60. Cf. Baudelaire:

"Fourmillante cité, cité pleine de rêves,

"Où le spectre en plein jour raccroche le
    passant."

63. Cf. Inferno III, 55–57:

                "si lunga tratta
di gente, ch'io non avrei mai creduto
che morte tanta n'avesse disfatta."

64. Cf. Inferno IV, 25–27:

"Quivi, secondo che per ascoltare,
"non avea pianto, ma' che di sospiri,
"che l'aura eterna facevan tremare."

68. A phenomenon which I have often
noticed.

74. Cf. the Dirge in Webster's *White Devil.*

76. V. Baudelaire, Preface to *Fleurs du Mal.*

II. A GAME OF CHESS

77. Cf. *Antony and Cleopatra*, II, ii, l. 190.

92. Laquearia. V. *Aeneid*, I, 726:

       dependent lychni laquearibus aureis
incensi, et noctem flammis funalia vincunt.

98. Sylvan scene. V. Milton, *Paradise Lost*, IV, 140.

99. V. Ovid, *Metamorphoses*, VI, Philomela.

100. Cf. Part III l. 204.

115. Cf. Part III l. 195.

118. Cf. Webster: "Is the wind in that door still?"

126. Cf. Part I l. 37, 48.

138. Cf. the game of chess in Middleton's *Women beware Women*.

III. THE FIRE SERMON

176. V. Spenser, *Prothalamion*.

192. Cf. *The Tempest*, I, ii.

196. Cf. Day, *Parliament of Bees:*

"When of the sudden, listening, you shall hear,
"A noise of horns and hunting, which shall bring
"Actaeon to Diana in the spring,
"Where all shall see her naked skin . . ."

197. Cf. Marvell, *To His Coy Mistress*.

199. I do not know the origin of the ballad from which these lines are taken; it was reported to me from Sydney, Australia.

202. V. Verlaine, *Parsifal*.

210. The currants were quoted at a price "carriage and insurance free to London"; and the Bill of Lading etc. were to be handed to the buyer upon payment of the sight draft.

218. Tiresias, although a mere spectator and not indeed a "character," is yet the most important personage in the poem, uniting all the rest. Just as the one-eyed merchant, seller of currants, melts into the Phoenician Sailor, and the latter is not wholly distinct from Ferdinand Prince of Naples, so all the women are one woman, and the two sexes meet in Tiresias. What Tiresias *sees*, in fact, is the substance of the poem. The whole passage from Ovid is of great anthropological interest:

. . . Cum Iunone iocos et maior vestra profecto est

Quam, quae contingit maribus', dixisse,
    'voluptas.'
Illa negat; placuit quae sit sententia docti
Quaerere Tiresiae: venus huic erat utraque
    nota.
Nam duo magnorum viridi coeuntia silva
Corpora serpentum baculi violaverat ictu
Deque viro factus, mirabile, femina septem
Egerat autumnos; octavo rursus eosdem
Vidit et 'est vestrae si tanta potentia plagae,'
Dixit 'ut auctoris sortem in contraria mutet,
Nunc quoque vos feriam!' percussis anguibus
    isdem
Forma prior rediit genetivaque venit imago.
Arbiter hic igitur sumptus de lite iocosa
Dicta Iovis firmat; gravius Saturnia iusto
Nec pro materia fertur doluisse suique
Iudicis aeterna damnavit lumina nocte,
At pater omnipotens (neque enim licet inrita
    cuiquam
Facta dei fecisse deo) pro lumine adempto
Scire futura dedit poenamque levavit honore.

   221. This may not appear as exact as

Sappho's lines, but I had in mind the "long-shore" or "dory" fisherman, who returns at nightfall.

253. V. Goldsmith, the song in *The Vicar of Wakefield*.

257. V. *The Tempest*, as above.

264. The interior of St. Magnus Martyr is to my mind one of the finest among Wren's interiors. See *The Proposed Demolition of Nineteen City Churches:* (P. S. King & Son Ltd.).

266. The Song of the (three) Thames-daughters begins here. From line 292 to 306 inclusive they speak in turn. V. *Götterdämmerung*, III, i: the Rhinedaughters.

279. V. Froude, *Elizabeth* Vol. I, ch. iv, letter of De Quadra to Philip of Spain:
"In the afternoon we were in a barge, watching the games on the river. (The queen) was alone with Lord Robert and myself on the poop, when they began to talk nonsense, and went so far that Lord Robert at last said, as I was on the spot there was no reason why they should not be married if the queen pleased."

293. Cf. *Purgatorio*, V. 133:

"Ricorditi di me, che son la Pia;

"Siena mi fe', disfecemi Maremma."

307. V. St. Augustine's *Confessions:* "to Carthage then I came, where a cauldron of unholy loves sang all about mine ears."

308. The complete text of the Buddha's Fire Sermon (which corresponds in importance to the Sermon on the Mount) from which these words are taken, will be found translated in the late Henry Clarke Warren's *Buddhism in Translation* (Harvard Oriental Series). Mr. Warren was one of the great pioneers of Buddhist studies in the occident.

312. From St. Augustine's *Confessions* again. The collocation of these two representatives of eastern and western asceticism, as the culmination of this part of the poem, is not an accident.

V. WHAT THE THUNDER SAID

In the first part of Part V three themes are employed: the journey to Emmaus, the approach to the Chapel Perilous (see Miss Weston's book) and the present decay of eastern Europe.

357. This is *Turdus aonalaschkae pallasii*, the hermit-thrush which I have heard in Quebec County. Chapman says (*Handbook of Birds of Eastern North America*) "it is most at home in secluded woodland and thickety retreats. . . . Its notes are not remarkable for variety or volume, but in purity and sweetness of tone and exquisite modulation they are unequaled." Its "water-dripping song" is justly celebrated.

360. The following lines were stimulated by the account of one of the Antarctic expeditions (I forget which, but I think one of Shackleton's): it was related that the party of explorers, at the extremity of their strength,

had the constant delusion that there was *noe more member* than could actually be counted.

366–76. Cf. Hermann Hesse, *Blick ins Chaos:* "Schon ist halb Europa, schon ist zumindest der halbe Osten Europas auf dem Wege zum Chaos, fährt betrunken im heiligem Wahn am Abgrund entlang und singt dazu, singt betrunken und hymnisch wie Dmitri Karamasoff sang. Ueber diese Lieder lacht der Bürger beleidigt, der Heilige und Seher hört sie mit Tränen."

401. "Datta, dayadhvam, damyata" (Give, sympathise, control). The fable of the meaning of the Thunder is found in the *Brihada-ranyaka — Upanishad*, 5, 1. A translation is found in Deussen's *Sechzig Upanishads des Veda*, p. 489.

407. Cf. Webster, *The White Devil*, V. vi:

". . . they'll remarry
Ere the worm pierce your winding-sheet, ere the spider
Make a thin curtain for your epitaphs."

411. Cf. *Inferno*, XXXIII, 46:

"ed io sentii chiavar l'uscio di sotto
all'orribile torre."

Also F. H. Bradley, *Appearance and Reality*,
p. 346.
"My external sensations are no less private to
myself than are my thoughts or my feelings.
In either case my experience falls within my
own circle, a circle closed on the outside; and,
with all its elements alike, every sphere is
opaque to the others which surround it. . . .
In brief, regarded as an existence which
appears in a soul, the whole world for each is
peculiar and private to that soul."

424. V. Weston: *From Ritual to Romance;*
chapter on the Fisher King.

427. V. *Purgatorio*, XXVI, 148.

"'Ara vos prec, per aquella valor
'que vos guida al som de l'escalina,
'sovegna vos a temps de ma dolor.'
Poi s'ascose nel foco che gli affina."

428. V. *Pervigilium Veneris*. Cf. Philomela
in Parts II and III.

429. V. Gerard de Nerval, Sonnet *El Desdichado*.

431. V. Kyd's *Spanish Tragedy*.

433. Shantih. Repeated as here, a formal ending to an Upanishad. "The Peace which passeth understanding" is a feeble translation of the content of this word.

CPSIA information can be obtained
at www.ICGtesting.com
Printed in the USA
LVHW100719141221
705979LV00019B/2235

9 781614 274315